AF228182

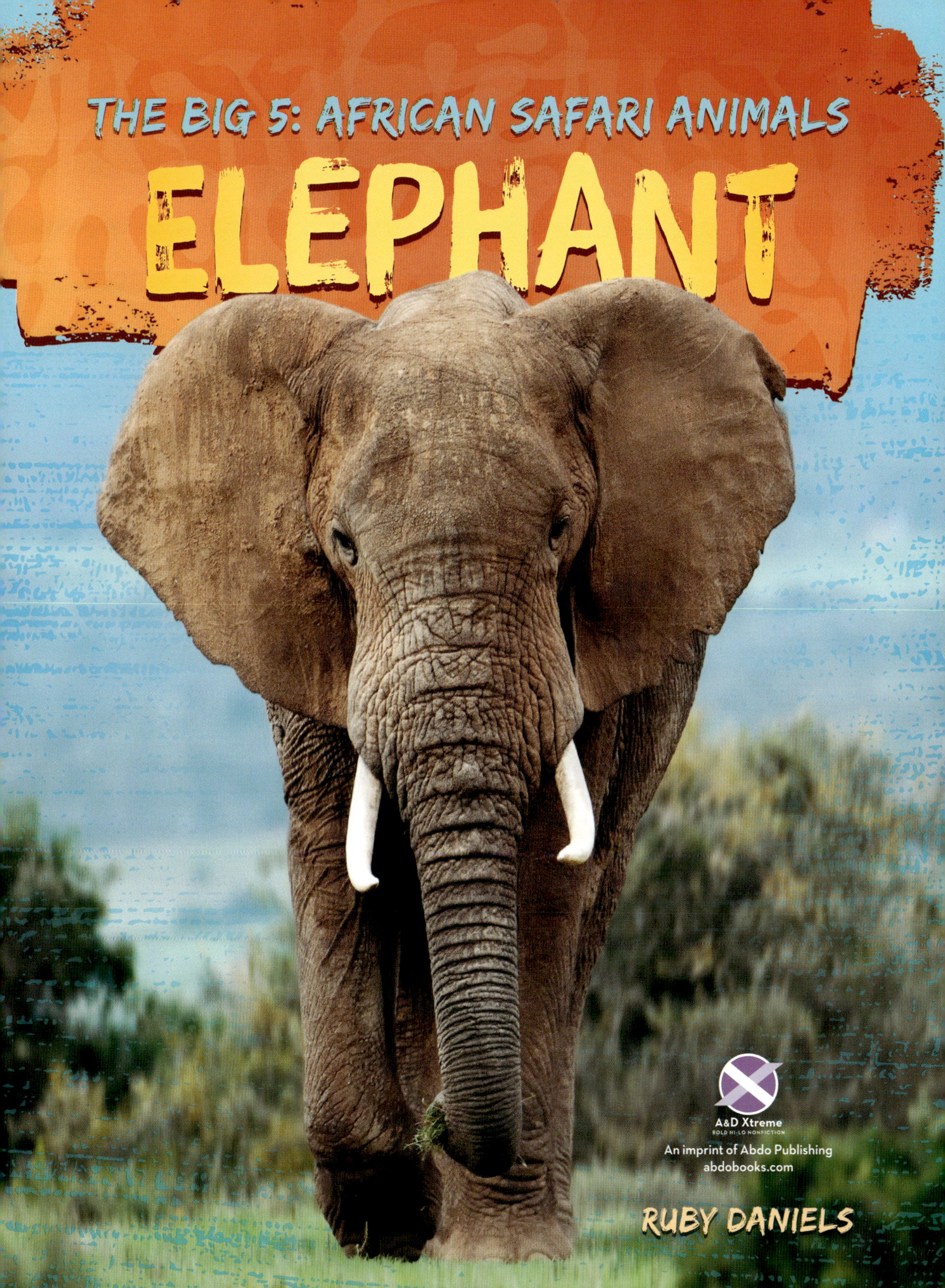

THE BIG 5: AFRICAN SAFARI ANIMALS
ELEPHANT
A&D Xtreme
BOLD HI-LO NONFICTION
An imprint of Abdo Publishing
abdobooks.com
RUBY DANIELS

TAKE IT TO THE XTREME!

GET READY FOR AN EXTREME ADVENTURE!
THE PAGES OF THIS BOOK WILL TAKE YOU INTO
THE THRILLING WORLD OF ICONIC AFRICAN ANIMALS.
WHEN YOU HAVE FINISHED READING THIS BOOK, TAKE THE
XTREME CHALLENGE ON PAGE 45 ABOUT WHAT YOU'VE LEARNED!

ABDOBOOKS.COM

Published by Abdo Publishing, a division of ABDO, PO Box 398166, Minneapolis, Minnesota 55439.
Copyright © 2026 by Abdo Consulting Group, Inc. International copyrights reserved in all countries.
No part of this book may be reproduced in any form without written permission from the publisher.
A&D Xtreme™ is a trademark and logo of Abdo Publishing.
Printed in the United States of America, North Mankato, MN.
052025
092025

Design: Kelly Doudna, Mighty Media, Inc.
Production: Mighty Media, Inc.
Editor: Katherine Chu

Cover Photograph: peterfodor/Adobe Stock

Interior Photographs: Ajith Gunawardena/Shutterstock, pp. 30–31; Alif Lamb/Shutterstock, pp. 40–41; boulham/Shutterstock, pp. 38–39; CherylRamalho/Shutterstock, pp. 12–13; Dietmar Rauscher/Shutterstock, pp. 20–21; Ger Metselaar/Shutterstock, pp. 4–5; hansen.matthew.d/Shutterstock, pp. 34–35; kavram/Shutterstock, pp. 16–17, 32–33; Leon Marais/Shutterstock, pp. 14–15; Lucian Coman/Shutterstock, pp. 28–29; Michael Potter11/Shutterstock, pp. 22–23; peterfodor/Adobe Stock, p. 1; plavi011/Shutterstock, pp. 36–37; Roger de la Harpe/Shutterstock, p. 9; Sean Nel/Shutterstock, p. 44; Svetlana Foote/Shutterstock, pp. 26–27; Tau5/Shutterstock, p. 8; uliasomay/Shutterstock, pp. 6–7; Vaclav Sebek/Shutterstock, pp. 24–25; Volodymyr Burdiak/Shutterstock, pp. 18–19; Willyam Bradberry/Shutterstock, pp. 10–11; xamnesiacx84/Shutterstock, pp. 42–43

Design Elements: DGIM studio/Adobe Stock (distressed texture); Ografica/Adobe Stock (header background); Zebra Finch/Adobe Stock (header background)

LIBRARY OF CONGRESS CONTROL NUMBER: 2024948551
PUBLISHER'S CATALOGING-IN-PUBLICATION DATA
Names: Daniels, Ruby, author.
Title: Elephant / by Ruby Daniels
Description: Minneapolis, Minnesota : Abdo Publishing, 2026 | Series: The big 5: African safari animals | Includes online resources and index.
Identifiers: ISBN 9781098296315 (lib. bdg.) | ISBN 9798384917748 (ebook)
Subjects: LCSH: Elephants--Juvenile literature. | African elephant--Juvenile literature. | Big game animals--Africa--Juvenile literature. | Herbivores--Juvenile literature. | Safaris--Juvenile literature.
Classification: DDC 591.96--dc23

CONTENTS

CHAPTER 1

ELEPHANT EXPEDITION

On a safari in Botswana, you see a gray shape in the distant grass. As you get closer, you realize it is enormous! It's about as tall as two adult humans and longer than a car. It has large ears, a long trunk, and huge tusks. You've just spotted an African elephant!

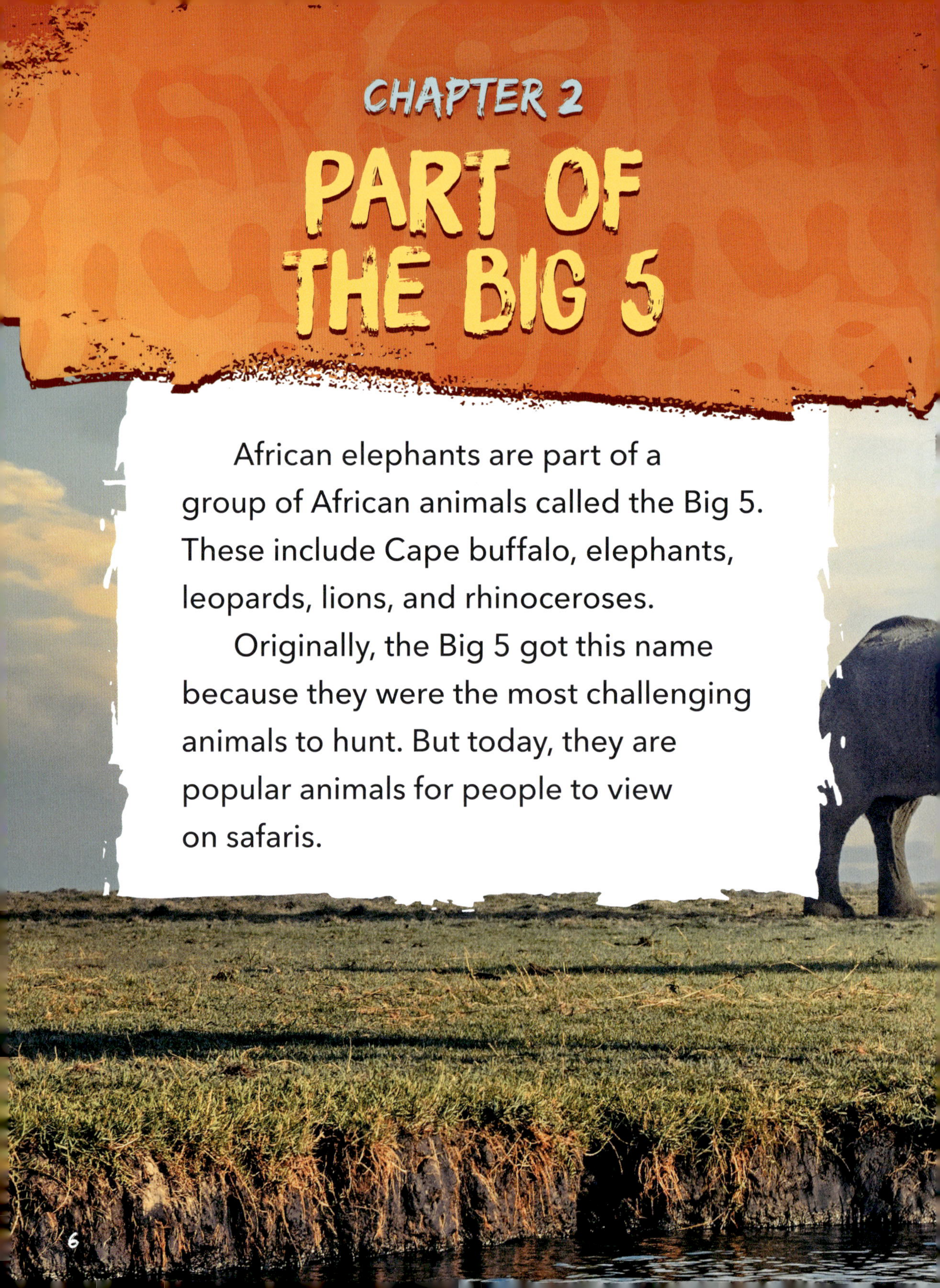

CHAPTER 2

PART OF THE BIG 5

African elephants are part of a group of African animals called the Big 5. These include Cape buffalo, elephants, leopards, lions, and rhinoceroses.

Originally, the Big 5 got this name because they were the most challenging animals to hunt. But today, they are popular animals for people to view on safaris.

African elephants are a keystone species. This means that without them, their ecosystem would change a lot or stop existing altogether.

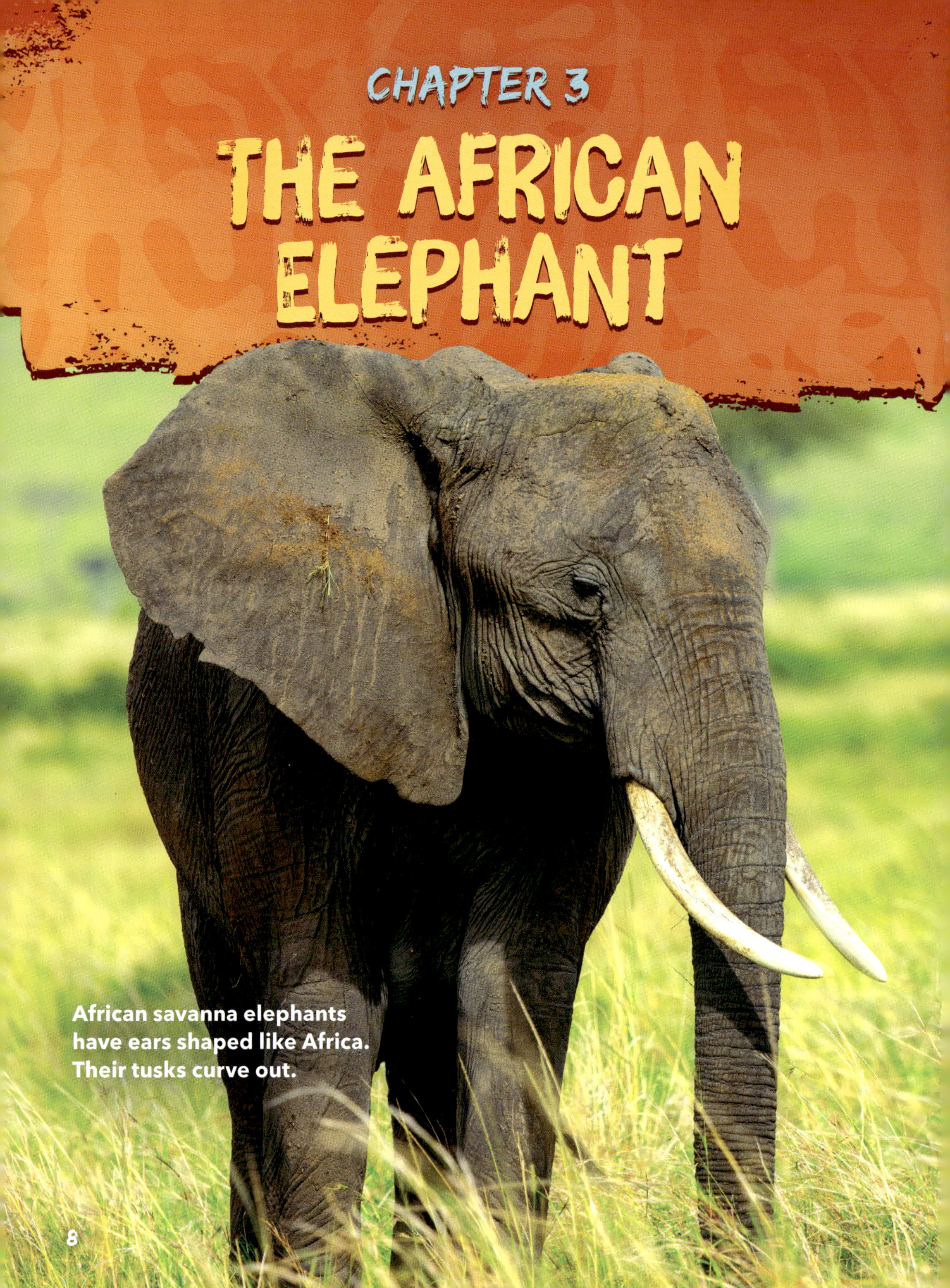

CHAPTER 3

THE AFRICAN ELEPHANT

African savanna elephants have ears shaped like Africa. Their tusks curve out.

There are two types of African elephants, the African **savanna** elephant and the African forest elephant. The savanna elephant is the largest land animal on Earth. It stands up to 13 feet (4 m) tall at the shoulder. It weighs up to 7 tons (6.4 t). The forest elephant stands up to 10 feet (3 m) tall at the shoulder. It weighs up to 6 tons (5.4 t).

African elephants like to
swim and can use their
trunk like a snorkel.

African elephants have a trunk, which is a long nose. Elephants use their trunk to breathe, smell, and communicate. They also use their trunk to suck up water to drink or shower themselves.

XTREME FACT

Elephants can grab objects with their trunk. An elephant's trunk has two fingerlike features on the end to help do this.

African elephants have big ears. They flap their ears to keep their bodies cool. Their ears also have blood vessels that circulate and cool down their blood.

African elephants have tusks. These are long teeth. Elephants dig for food and water with their tusks. They also use their tusks to remove tree bark from trees to eat.

XTREME FACT

Elephants have dominant tusks like humans have dominant hands. This means elephants can be left- or right-tusked.

Male elephants usually have larger tusks and will use them to fight each other.

African elephants
can solve problems
and use tools.

Elephants are known for their intelligence. They understand pointing and can recognize themselves in a mirror. Elephants also have long memories. They can remember places and other elephants they've met before.

XTREME FACT

African elephants' brains weigh about 11 pounds (5 kg). That is almost four times larger than human brains.

CHAPTER 4

LIFE AS AN AFRICAN ELEPHANT

XTREME FACT

Elephants have the longest **gestation** period of any **mammal**. It is about 22 months long.

African elephants live in herds made of females and young male elephants. The oldest female, called the **matriarch**, leads the herd. **Savanna** elephants live in herds of up to 70 elephants. Forest elephants live in herds of up to 20 elephants. Adult males usually live alone or in small groups with other males. They only meet with females to mate.

As their names suggest, **savanna** elephants live on the savanna and forest elephants live in the forest. Savanna elephants live in regions south of the African Sahara Desert. They live in all areas except for the rainforests. Forest elephants live in the rainforests of Central and West Africa.

The African savanna elephant is also called the African bush elephant.

Elephants sleep an average of two hours a day. They can even sleep standing up! To do this, they may lean against a tree or rock.

African elephants are **herbivores**. They eat grass, tree bark, fruit, and other plants. They can eat up to 375 pounds (170 kg) of food and drink about 50 gallons (189 L) of water each day. They **forage** for most of the day and night.

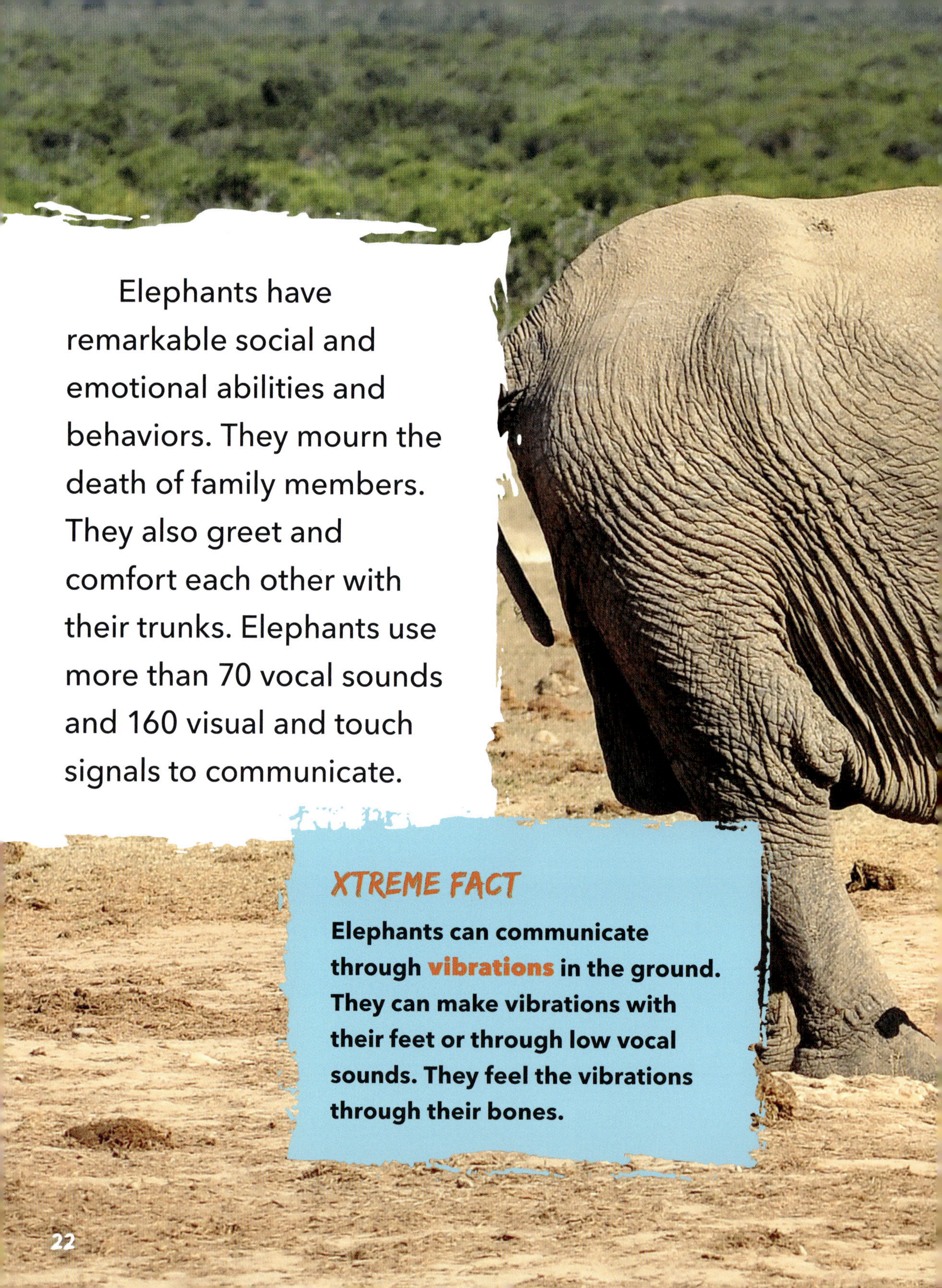

Elephants have remarkable social and emotional abilities and behaviors. They mourn the death of family members. They also greet and comfort each other with their trunks. Elephants use more than 70 vocal sounds and 160 visual and touch signals to communicate.

XTREME FACT

Elephants can communicate through **vibrations** in the ground. They can make vibrations with their feet or through low vocal sounds. They feel the vibrations through their bones.

Elephants will help other elephants
that are stuck or injured.

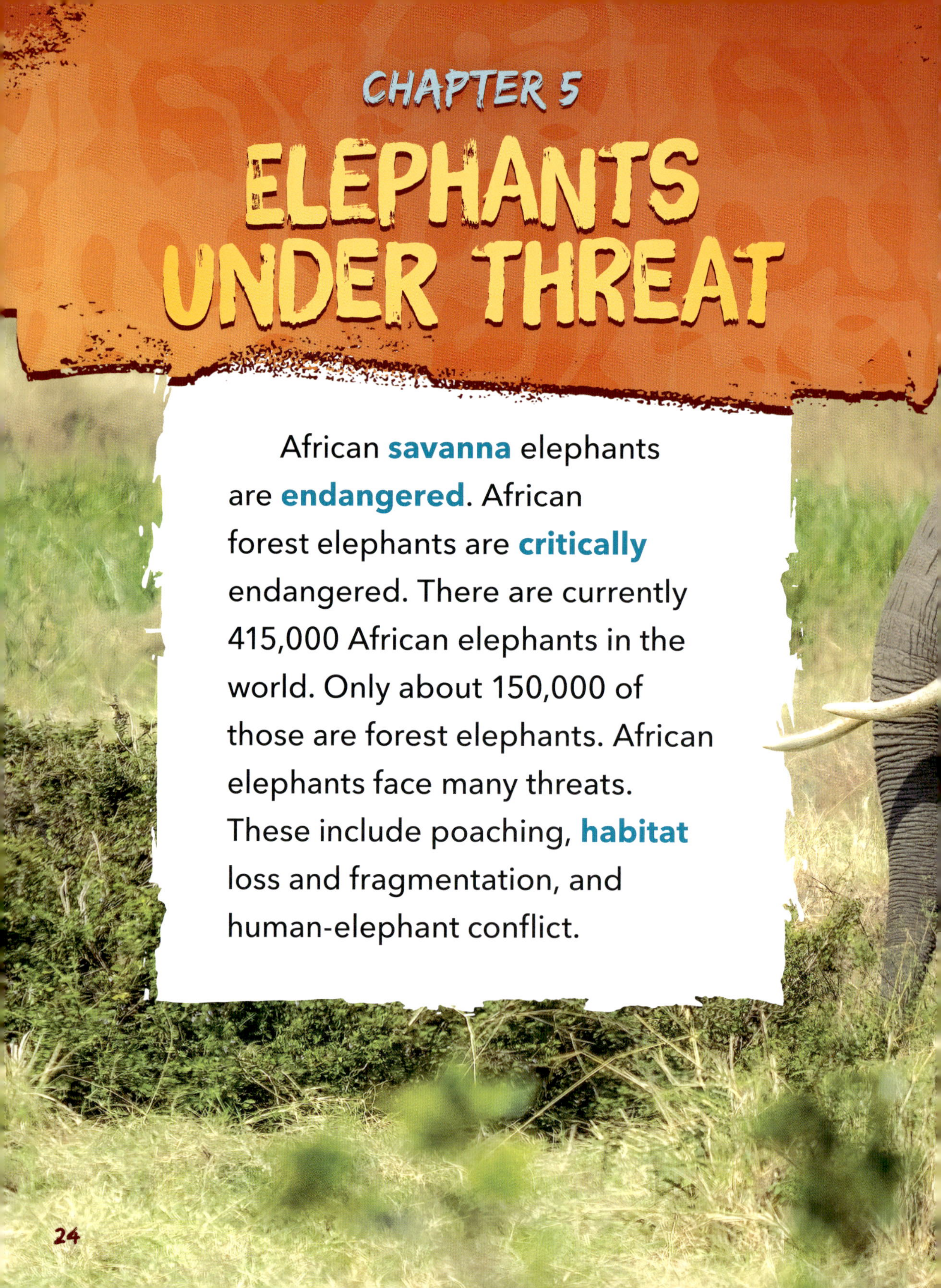

CHAPTER 5

ELEPHANTS UNDER THREAT

African **savanna** elephants are **endangered**. African forest elephants are **critically** endangered. There are currently 415,000 African elephants in the world. Only about 150,000 of those are forest elephants. African elephants face many threats. These include poaching, **habitat** loss and fragmentation, and human-elephant conflict.

Female elephants usually have a baby every three to six years. Poaching and other threats harm elephants faster than they can reproduce.

Poaching is illegal hunting. People poach elephants for the ivory in their tusks. Poachers kill more than 17,000 elephants a year for ivory.

There is an **international** ban on trading elephant ivory. Many countries have banned elephant ivory markets. But some countries still allow the sale of ivory. And people still **smuggle** and sell it illegally.

Some people call ivory "white gold" and view it as a symbol of wealth. Others think wearing ivory can protect them from bad luck or harm.

People take over
land when creating new
buildings and systems.
This causes **habitat** loss
and fragmentation.

Habitat loss is when
the size of an animal's
habitat is reduced. Habitat
fragmentation is when an
animal's habitat is broken
up. Both result in less land
for elephants to survive on.

Habitat fragmentation separates elephant groups from each other. This makes it harder for the groups to breed.

With smaller **habitats**, elephants may **forage** on farms. This leads to elephants damaging crops or hurting humans. Humans may hunt elephants to stop the animals. This is called human-elephant conflict.

Electric fencing is one of the
most used ways in the world to
block off land from wild animals.
People in Africa use it to prevent
human-elephant conflict.

CHAPTER 6

ESSENTIAL ANIMALS

Birds may sit on elephants to eat bugs off their skin and hair and get a ride to another location.

The loss of African elephants is a serious issue. African elephants are important for the survival of other **species** in their **ecosystem**. There are many ways that elephants shape their **habitats**.

African elephants dig for water with their tusks. Other animals can drink this water. Elephants eat many different plants and trees. They spread seeds through their dung. Elephants clear paths in the forest and keep trees out of the **savanna**. Other animals use these paths and open areas.

XTREME FACT

An elephant's footprint can fill with water. This creates a tiny **ecosystem** for tadpoles and other living creatures.

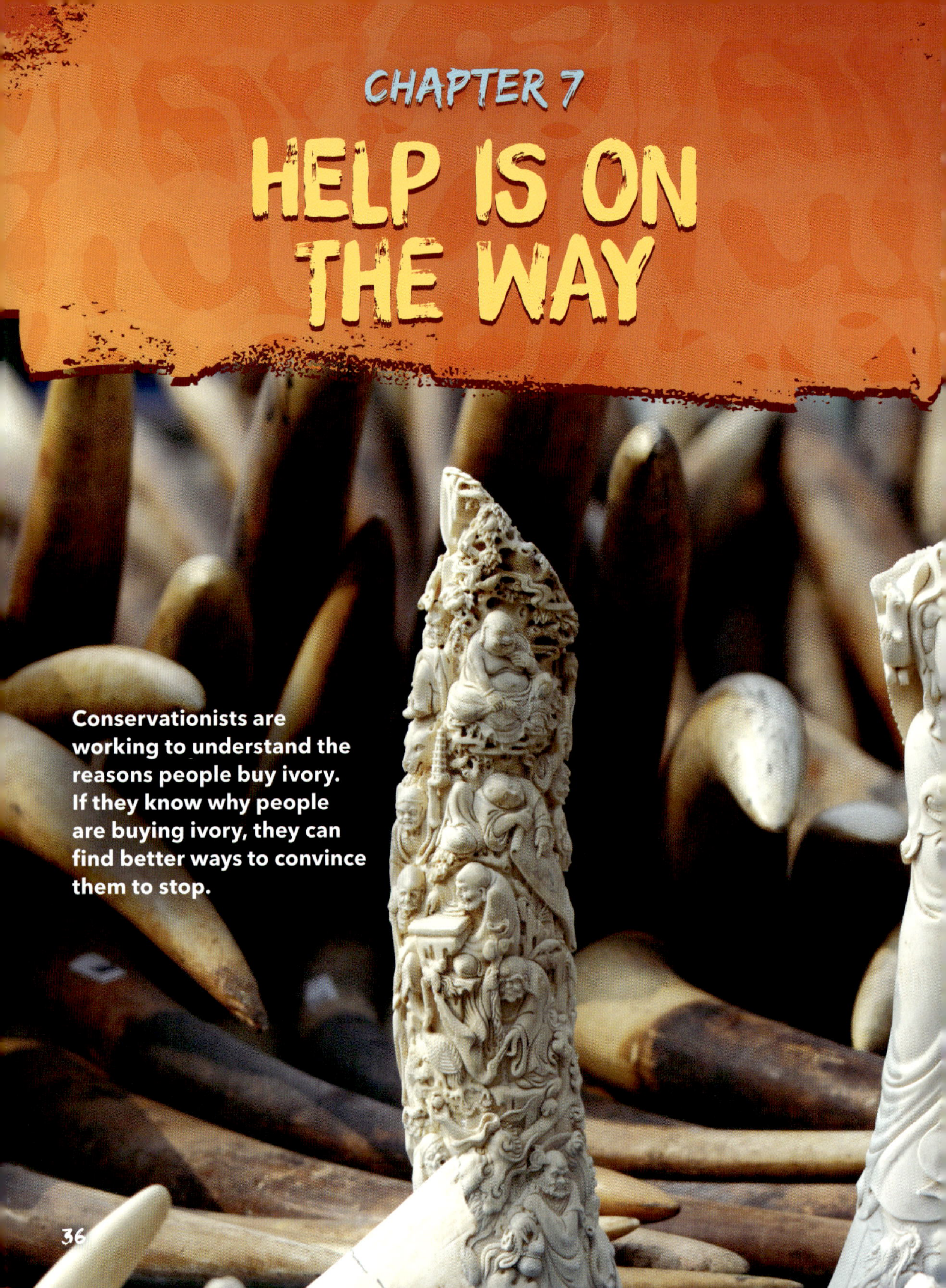

CHAPTER 7

HELP IS ON THE WAY

Conservationists are working to understand the reasons people buy ivory. If they know why people are buying ivory, they can find better ways to convince them to stop.

Conservationists work hard to protect African elephants. Organizations try to lower the **demand** for ivory. They explain the effect on elephants. They remind people that trading elephant ivory is illegal in many countries. And organizations work with other countries' governments to close elephant ivory markets.

Some organizations attempt to prevent **habitat** loss and human-elephant conflict. They set up and manage protected areas for elephants. This helps keep elephants away from humans.

Other organizations educate and include people in **conservation** efforts. They encourage people to find ways to keep elephants away from farms instead of killing them.

XTREME FACT

The Save the Elephants organization helps set up beehive fences around farms. Elephants avoid the bees, keeping them away from crops.

CHAPTER 8

FAN FAVORITES

African elephants are popular animals to view on safaris. They are very big and have many unusual features. People can watch exciting scenes like baby elephants playing or adult elephants fighting. And people might even see elephants use their trunks to shower.

People may see elephants shower themselves with dust. This keeps them cool and protects their skin from the sun on hot days.

A day in Chobe National Park usually includes a morning and afternoon safari. The safari can take place by car or boat.

African elephants are common in many countries in Africa. Botswana has more elephants than any other country. Its Chobe National Park is a popular safari **destination**. Zimbabwe, South Africa, and many other countries also offer national parks for elephant viewing.

CHAPTER 9

MORE TO EXPLORE

African elephants are awe-inspiring. Their size, features, intelligence, and more make them special. Though elephants face many threats, **conservationists** work hard to preserve their **habitats** and protect them. Animal lovers can go on a wildlife safari and enjoy these grand creatures in their natural habitats.

African elephant herds can travel through 37 different countries in Africa.

XTREME CHALLENGE

**TAKE THE QUIZ BELOW AND
PUT WHAT YOU'VE LEARNED TO THE TEST!**

1) What qualities make elephants special?

2) How do elephants communicate with each other?

3) Why are elephants important to other animals in their environment?

4) How are conservation organizations helping to reduce elephant poaching?

5) Would you want to see elephants on a safari? Why or why not?

GLOSSARY

conservation–the planned management of natural resources or animals to protect them from damage or destruction. People who do this are conservationists.

critical–at a point of high risk.

demand–the amount of an available product that buyers are willing and able to purchase.

destination–a place someone is going to or something is sent to.

dominant–one of two of the same body parts that is used more often or is more effective.

ecosystem–a community of organisms and their surroundings.

endangered–in danger of becoming extinct.

forage–to search for food.

gestation–the carrying of a developing unborn baby in the uterus.

habitat–a place where a living thing is naturally found.

herbivore–an animal that eats only plants.

mammal—a warm-blooded animal that has hair and whose females produce milk to feed their young.

matriarch—a female who oversees and rules a family or group.

savanna—a grassy plain with few or no trees.

smuggle—to import or export something secretly and illegally.

species—a group of related living beings that can naturally produce offspring with each other.

vibration—very small, quick movements back and forth.

ONLINE RESOURCES

To learn more about African elephants, please visit **abdobooklinks.com** or scan this QR code. These links are routinely monitored and updated to provide the most current information available.

INDEX